811.52
Fer

86610

Fergusson.
Poems, 1929-1961.

Date Due

MAY 7 69			

The Library

Nazareth College of Rochester, N. Y.

PRINTED IN U.S.A.

POEMS

POEMS

1929–1961

by FRANCIS FERGUSSON

RUTGERS UNIVERSITY PRESS

New Brunswick, New Jersey

Copyright © 1962 by Rutgers, The State University

Library of Congress Catalogue Card Number: 62-10823

Manufactured in the United States of America

Acknowledgment is made to the following periodicals, in which some of these poems were first published:

Anthologist (Rutgers)

New Directions (1937 and 1938)

Partisan Review

Poetry

Sewanee Review

The four lines from "I Surrender, Dear," by Gordon Clifford and Harry Barris, copyright 1931, Mills Music Co., are quoted on pages 18–19 with the permission of the copyright owner.

CONTENTS

v

PENELOPE, A Theater Lyric (1945) 45

POEMS, 1945–1960

POEMS

TO THE MEMORY OF MARION CROWNE FERGUSSON

ON THE TURNING EARTH

I

Here in our time, on the turning earth,
Nightfall or another day
May restore the sense of a life that is gone,
But time itself goes all one way.

Dreaming words from the human past
May reach our misery, but I heard
"Her spirit has not left you, and
She sees all things in the light of God"

As the chill cry of need, when I,
Missing her touch, her voice, her face,
Like any animal bereaved
Turned and turned in the empty place.

Now, as light grows or dims with dusk
And that blinded time comes back, I seek
In remorse, in the sense of her presence lost,
Something to say, something to keep
        In what time is left on the turning earth.

II

I would turn, at nightfall, if I could,
As though she were there, in another room,
Or waiting in the silent house
With the porch light on for my return,

To near her spirit where it lived
Beside me, on our way together,

3

Must close, and yet unknown, unknown,
Loved mystery that made my weather.

But in the quick play of memory
Loved faces change as they appear,
Infant or child, woman or man;
And I cannot really see or hear

In that mortal game of hide and seek
Her eager spirit, that could give
To the vanishing actuality
All her passionate need to live

As though for all eternity;
I only know that, so, she wove
The lasting dream of the family
With the intelligence of love,

And we did not fear mortality
As we closed, together, a house we'd known,
Or said good-by to the children when
It was time for them to set out from home.

After thirty years, in quiet, free;
In the spring light, in the clear weather,
The thought of death somewhere ahead
Brought us, contented, more near together;

But here in time that goes one way
As in that time, so near its end,
The ultimate actuality
That I can neither see nor mend

Burns black within me as I know
Our past all past, our future gone,

See her, although so close, most far,
Although so near, most near, alone.

III

When the turning of the earth brings another day,
And the actual scene is clear to the eye,
From blackness burning within me I
Would turn, if I could see the way.

But the visible city where our time
Most burns in actuality,
Where I sensed her opening spirit sense
Infinite possibility;

The city crowds where she loved to linger
Absorbed, like an innocent child at gaze,
Yet alert to the cruel agility
Of the city's gamble, the city's games,
    Are become a scene I can only see
    Beyond the glass of a train window.

Seen, unseen, the receding city
On its countless ways, with its countless schemes,
That lived beneath actuality
More real than its flicker of bodiless dreams,

When in her living being she
Unsealed the speeding glass of youth
With her mortal touch, her real response,
Miraculous clue to music, truth;

When we were one, and felt at one
With unseen millions on the way
Where past and future made harmony:
For she, as though knowing the end of the way

In the city that so long had been
Her loved antagonist, destiny,
Undeluded, patiently,
Could die, as the light of day for me
    Burned black in that actuality.

The human spirit cannot see
In actuality alone,
Where past and future both are gone,
Life and mortality are one.

I cannot see or live where she
Who was easily hurt as a child unwove
Her woman's being, treasure on earth,
The precious motive, the strong knot of love.
    Can neither see nor turn away
    While in time itself that goes one way
    Her life recedes all silently.

IV

The slowly widening light of spring,
Earlier darkness, the first frost,
Return in silence, and silent is
What I would keep, though she is lost.

Not the voluble city of our time,
Nor murmur of the heedless flesh,
Nor words of terror, nor words of faith,
But the sense of the truth of her spirit is

What I would keep, and can only have
In human piety, remorse
For the silence of one being lost
Without all remedy. But because

I cannot turn with the murderous word
"What is without all remedy
Must be without regard," I give
To her still beckoning memory

My clumsy words. In them she heard
Tentative echoes of the theme
That she could hear without a word:
The truth of the human spirit's need
    Under its dreams of life and death
    In the remote recorded past,
    And here in our time, on the turning earth.

POEMS, 1929–1938

FROM A BOY'S TRAVELOGUE

I

Dark island airs, soft fog,
Rumble of Russell Square, odor of coal:
Can this be memory, which is so strange
And yet familiar?
Receding on high London wheels, and I on foot,
The soul of London like a muscle-bound old man,
    behind
The motionless big house-fronts blackened with fog.

II

Monsieur Mandarin of reproachful eyes,
Piratical smile and courteous lies,
Was master of ceremonies; subdued
To the demands of centuries of tact
He in a drawing room could always act
Smooth. I felt my eyes swim and my heart fail
He was so friendly in his swallowtail
Under the luster in his splendid lair
Of many mirrors brilliantly aware.

III

At Fiesole, soft at the Bedloes', in
Steam heat, among Madonna lillies,
I marveled at the dogma of
The fierce late painters:
The rocky hill, the Cross, the empty sky:
HUMANI GENERIS REDEMPTORI: below,
The broken columns, Rome or Troy.

IV

Come follow sly Odysseus speeding home,
Safe in the swift Phaeacians' ocean-coursing ship;

Yield to that sweet sleep which is almost death,
Almost the womb-sleep that precedes a birth,
As if the loud, cold boiling of the sea under the stern
Were heat that could refine you, and the prow foresaw
Your secret being by the sea made new.

—Came Butterworth Parker of Brattle Street,
And said, "Amusing about these field glasses.
When I came abroad I decided to rent a pair,
Thinking it would be cheaper.
Then Ainslee persuaded me to stay a month longer,
And now I wish I'd bought a pair outright . . .
Oh, dear . . . though I'd hardly have much use for
    them
In Cambridge. Excuse me a moment:
On English boats I make a habit
Of bicarbonate of soda."

V

Under the mist the clear gray wave
Smoothly laves the water line.
Bells and voices in mist are grave.
(Those voices were there all the time.)

Passing the white Bay Islands' sand
The bright Bay breeze, *cantabile*,
Freshens "the clean-haired Yankee land,"
Brings the soft ghost of the Fourth of July.

Do the sweet heavens love the old?
From Bunker Hill to Barnegat Bay
On beach porches the "hairless old"
Preserve the white form of another day,

While the harbor life beneath the smokes
Of dumps, Far Rockaway to Jersey,
Is burning along the ruined coast
In alien heat, in mystery.

The spines of its back hunch the sky.
Ah, silly wedding cake of lead:
In the tender sky a stony Sunday.
The vertical fields of glass are dead.

Bells and gongs in the morning air!
Echoes and smells, remembered things:
Beyond the sea this life was there.
Now the ship, throbbing, swings, it swings

Hurrah! to glide the landing stage,
The populace and packing cases
And the straw hats (hurrah) and oranges,
The chewing gum, soft shirts, and spread pink faces.

Green lapping tide . . . south to these lands . . .
The easy Negroes line the docks,
George Washington spits on his hands,
Gets set to handle the trucks.

"Now my charms are all o'erthrown
And what strength I have's mine own,"
On the beach a pumice stone:
The sea is deaf and this is home.

VI

When the train jolted to a stop
In the bricked depot, by the sand hill,

13

Time jolted to a stop.
The train bell made the air acutely still.

A stopped watch can add nothing to the tick
Of the old friends' desert voices,
Unwilling waking, and
Heart's intermittence: the familiar voice
    Of Doc
On the porch behind the picket fence
    A-rock:
Joe Martin: Drugs & Soda: Doc.

—Remember Morton, do you? He went to pot;
His nature, I guess. . . . Found 'im in the vacant lot
Behind the shed.
          So near?
                   When they find a friend
They lose their fear.

              "I, a child, very old"
Without surprise resuffering
"The growth by the margins of pondwaters" of
"The simple soul that knows nothing."

It is the timeless mind that knows
When the soul, unsprung,
Runs down the death grooves.

VII

O Muse, just as the five-fifty
Runs down and stops, with good-night jokes,
Diminish to the certainty
Of the Eternal Home Folks.

Puncture your fear with kind pity,
Laughter with grave last thoughts, and say
Whence comes the small necessity
So to end your day?

You had thought to sing of Antony,
Of how his bright star rose and fell.
But here in the flesh is Uncle Cleary:
You are weary and he knows you well.

POEMS, 1929–1938

CITY SCENES

ANTIQUE TALE

The shrewd Manahattoes and chattering taxis
Are busy eternally with new business.
Under the spring-dim cliffs, the echoing glass,
The restless tribes wheel "westward from Paradise,"
Skeptic and urgent; wheeling.

There, in the fifth-month evening, you may see
Jim Sweetland prowl, round-eyed and bony-jawed,
An intellectual journalist
        In town for the week end
With a shave n'-a-haircut
        Serious
And in fine health. A bird dog smells of hound,
And Sweetland of Bay Rum, as he points the dusk.
—Here in the Village he leans, intent, to state—
Plenty fine girls 'll letcha take their pants off—
Leaning; expedient.

"An isle, Ogygia, lies far off in the sea."

And in that evening you may see
How Josie Schmalz, uncertain, welcoming,
Forgets the lonely cries of kikes and goys.
And she will scream: Do you know you're fresh?—
        then coo:
But I shouldn't talk, I'm a fresh person too. . . .
Excuse me, you remind me of a guy
I knew at CCNY. . . . Well, are you shocked?
        He used to say,
Josie, no person's more gracious then you—
        I may seem proud
I may seem gay
        It's just a pose

It's not my way
        I surrender, dear.

Wanna wanna wanna wanna wanna
Wanna. Dishevelment of feathers, sighing.
"After the big flight from the coast,
Crooner—Flicker Lass imbroglio;
The mags are clamoring."

From the soothed small hours the turning world
                evolves
The dawn. Across the burning trash piles, feel
The salt wind blowing on the prairie,
The prairie breathing-in the sea, across
The littered fire escapes.

        Ulysses faintly wept
For his lost human mate;
        Purged Sweetland flees
His health relieved
        And spirit spent

While Uncle Suburb's wavering shape regains
Number two five eight two Ninety-Second Avenue
And Aunt Eclampsia, in the soot-filmed light.

Without-you-I-can't-make-my
                way . . .

MRS. WHITE

"Like cures like, and for this hunt my malady becomes my most
desired health."—*Moby Dick*.

Through the disordered drawing room, in the winter
    light,
Came Mrs. White, with one hand pushing her hair,
With the other offering absent-minded greeting:
"I have been trying to live to myself here,"
She whispered to the ceiling: "the sensitive, inner
    thing."

I thought of Mary Baker Eddy, sick to death,
Aspiring still, chill-rapt Bostonienne,
Above the sour smoke of Boston and Lynn,
Her eyes gone out, but under white curls
Her intuitive antennae feeling
Her "sweet deific principle" . . .

                    "I have been feeding
On Emerson's mind. He is just like you.
Visible things are not all of life;
Do you feel it too?"

NIGHT CLUB

The fourteen calcimined houris say *da-da* in time to
    the music,
Clapping their baby-palms, prancing their tails of red
    feathers;
And Miss Mann-Hippo, Infanta of the Coal Kingdom,
Laughs till she shakes like a bowl of good-fella.

But she tires quickly, begins to pout, is trundled
— How can she bear it? — whining
To her clean hospital on the Hudson, victim
Of her maid, chauffeur, and companion, grave-faced
    ascetics,
Who remember that grandpa made money.

INTELLECTUAL NOURISHMENT

Professor James Russell Emerson Parker
Scratches nimbly for his flock of intelligent ladies,
Points nourishing grains for their brilliant pecking,
Contented ca-talkling.

Fearing the din of their horrified squawking,
The blushing disorder of rumpled feathers,
Exposure to view of virginal stockings,
He is careful to keep their ca-talkling contented.

EUGENICS

The Nordic editor of *Man and Woman*
Plods after his fine big wife in Adultship,
His hand is heavy on her neck in Comradehood;
But little M. Hérissé,
Watching the elephant, Sardanapalus,
Followed by Mrs. Sardanapalus,
Her trunk, marching, swinging his friendly tail,
Envies the healthful turdfall of Sardanapalus.

THE BLUMENSCHEINS,
OR, LIEBE, AMOR, LOVE AND LIBIDO

When I took the Blumenscheins' upholstered lift
To visit their illness, the sunshine
Warmed through window glass. I offered them a gift
Of fresh-cut roses, hoping to buy off,

With familiar things, their poor hurt faces;
But they wanted me to see their daughter Katherine.
Past the soft places and the polished places
They tip-toed to the bedside of their tender passion;

Of their Liebe, which was *so* schön when it started
     out:
Ach! *industrious* Liebe, which should make all Ma-
     nahatta
Harmonious as shining Louis and his Braut!
Make Bruderschaft of Jahveh und Minnehaha!

From Louis' sportive bowels of compassion,
From Clara's satin ribbon things, with lace,
Came Liebe, as their little daughter Katherine,
As the rosy eternity of their flesh,

Now the image
Of its illness.

"We worry so about our Katherine."
Neither gigantic kindness, a ranch vacation,
Nor the rich comfort of the Marlborough-Blenheim
Could wake or wean her, in her puny generation.

Dormant through such winter, drifting to Wellesley,
Her finicky being first came alive

25

Among Whittier's red leaves, when she saw Jerry,
And Amor, waking, waked her to feed and thrive!

She gazed, "understanding" his stiff young gloom,
Thinking he would wake with a male cry of sur-
    prise,
Crave that hid "immensity in little room,"
Then be happily dandled in her love-blind eyes;

And the old folks smiled
So merry and so mild.

Well . . . The June the youngsters met in the
    Neckar Valley
Their green barbarism was a fine soft pasture
For *some* starved passion. . . . The band played in
    the Schloss Café.
But Harvard Jerry? What was "The Proper Gesture"

In those lands depraved, where he could not see
Why she must drain him, or else cry from her hurt
    throat,
His pain her food? —Between memory and memory
"Plaisir" must needs bud through the "Drang nach
    Tod."

She watched him try for dignity, "Love" metamor-
    phosed
To "Crise Morale," her will his fear, watched him say,
"We must consider the incident closed,"
Trying to break it off, her off, or pull away.

Came old folks's blush, their smiling grief
—Ts! *tiny* mystery! —Despair

(Tochter, öffne deinen Schoss!)
The night they offered them relief
With perfume in Katherine's hair,

Dinner and wine at the Schloss.
(Shh: old remedy no surcease
For Katherine and Jerry, where
Untouching young lay close.)

*

"We don't know what was the matter with that fella,"
Sagte Louis; "Shh," sagte Clara, "Be calm."
"She's so kind," sagte Louis, "With me und Clara!"
—The immensity shrunk to little room,

To a sickbed
In her bedroom.

There wise Medicine and Psychotherapy,
Distraction, gentle Enemas, a Milk Diet,
Laugh off the terrible epiphany
Of lost love, and waste it in the warm quiet.

THE CHARM

Harper cries; 'Tis time, 'Tis time:

Take window glass from a steam flat,
The cornea of a traffic light;

Pince-nez of an executive,
A punctured tire, a wire sieve.

Throw in the disregarded toy
Of babe that tests with cruel cry,

And puckered skin from grave forehead
When the nerve inside is dead;

Silently then add a few
Crimson threads from a plush pew,

And the long jaw of solemn young
Relaxed by bullet through the lung.

Cool it with a baboon's blood,
Then the charm is firm and good.

JOE

Avenue A is long. Joe Brennan waits
For "the first day of the first month of the first year."
He has a Comrade's slow grip, and candid Kansas
    eyes.
"When the Workers Take Control," he says softly,
"Fellas like you and me can live. . . . Then
We can get back to the woods again. . . . Have
    camp-fires."
He hitches his pants up, friendly. "Swim."

Avenue A is long. Proletcult
I cannot see. But I can see
Joe Brennan, Harry Spinks and Emma Bromberg,
Their troubled child-eyes bounded by the suburb.

AVENUE A CONSIDERED AS A TOMB

Therefore we live: though such a life we have
As but so many Mandrakes on his grave.
                    —Elegy on Prince Henry.

Afternoon silent as glass
In the bright Pax Americana:
"Pigeons on the grass, alas!"
And in the Rotogravure

John D.'s little eidolon
(Hero without imperium)
Blinks withered in the winsome sun
Of Ormond, its Elysium.

Who then creep out, unshaken
By Roman wheels, to play,
When he is gone who could waken
The Sabbath gigantic causeway?

—Ce ne sont pas des hommes, hélas!
Ce ne sont pas des femmes:
Pigeons on the grass, alas,
Ce sont des américains.

—But who is it this light sun breeds
From what has died, to Sunday shoes,
To discontent, here in the clean
North-warehouse-shadows' mortuary dews?

—The harmless *keres* of him,
Infesting the bones he left,
His powerhouses shut and dim.
We are free when we are bereft

Whom neither the iron derrick's
Impotency
Nor the black smokestack's
Claim of the sky
Nor our brief shadows'
Confluence in the still doorway
(And under the consenting death of gas tanks)
Can satisfy or destroy.

POEMS, 1929–1938

SIGNS OF THE ANCIENT FLAME

COLD-WEATHER NOTE

"High time to get to sea as soon as I can."—*Moby Dick.*

Like unspent children on short winter days,
Meeting the end of the day in the afternoon,
We met, denying that we met so soon,
In our missed season.

—If in the arctic sea-pause infancy grow old?
The sailor dreaming on the mast forget his hold,
Wake in the ocean?

        We had at least
That fear confirmed between us:
Two heatless flames that leaned to meet,
Helpless to reach
        "The fire that refines them."

CHIAROSCURO: SPRING

Out of the lamp-lit chrysalis, beloved, spring stars
    release
Throngs grateful for the darkness, freely winging
Through the diminished rumble, taxiing: hark to their
    cries!
Come, before the light changes. Pin these flowers.
    There are still skies.

All night my love and I shall consent to consenting
    eyes.

In our sweet trance the crowded town revolves,
The tumbled bed where the gift was spent, discarded
    flowers;
The fuming streets march blindly up with day,
What was given our freshened eyes is taken away:

The turning world does not belong to you and me.

Yet in the mind's eye, each
In his black case again, can see
(Bustling alone through smoky sunlight)
That I was given you in that vision, and you me.

CITY EPITHALAMIUM

The smoky star in purple west
Is rising, Hesperus Adest:
Now the fond lip to eager ear
Will soon be whispering "my dear,"
Graspers of darkness grasping wrong
Whom the Star moves in this year's throng.

But far beneath the influence
In the dim crowds, of Hesperus,
She is more deeply tugging you
With the dear bond that is her due;
Not to your dark nor Star's darkness,
Anonymous to anonymous.

Then say good-by (for now you must)
To gatherings in evening dust
Of all the vacant similar young
Whom you took form and grew among:
Past the viaduct in the west
Lone-burning Hesperus Adest;

And under the Evening Star's red course
(The track of antique Hesperus)
Her flushed head, bending, has confessed
What stiffed your back and burned your breast:
What soft destruction you avowed,
Open with her in the one wound.

MANNIKIN

March was shifting the season behind our glass,
Wind in the empty airshaft. What sacrifice
For the changing year? —the lonesome singing
Of a tenor crooner in our areaway:
> *Water-bo-o-oy, where are you hi-i-ding?*
> *Ef you doan come, gwine tell-a yo mam-my* . . .
Come! let us sing with him
                              And the tiny stones of the city!
—But your eyes, round with hurt, were fixing me,
Your dime rang on the damp cement,
The wind blew through the basement,
And your eyes did not grow softer, satisfied,
Till the little image of that crying mannikin
Diminished and perished.

SONG

Feel weather only, never speak
  Now while the weather pauses.
This is the grass we could not seek.
  Pause as the weather pauses,

All grateful now and virginal,
Humble and sly and animal.

Have sun in eye, not dream or love,
  And relinquish memory,
Eye iridescent as the dove
  And body silent near me.

THE HEAD OF THE WIFE

Clubfoot; if unblessed by wife or mother,
Yet not, after all, the unriddler,
What is he, in an "age of transition," but
"A stone rejected by the builder?"

Where he fell the still sun visits the village.
And homing to memory's eye, revision,
Intact the smiling horizon riddle, by
His solemn crimes uncaught, his missed distinctions:

Between machinery mastered and her love,
The wound of love and castration,
Charity, and a man's love for a woman;
The Furies' mockery and their true blessing. . . .

"Give a woman all and she has nothing,"
Though absorbed in the wondrous cradle,
The world well lost for such a bauble . . .
Or be blinded by this needle:

By the mirages and the desert wind
Of the unwilling Eumenides
For whom the "evidence of things not seen"
Is a feeble excuse.

Must, then, "believe"; content
To acknowledge "youthful error";
But in spite of the clear warning of maiming
Not guilty of murder;

Thirsty, at least, for the true spring, lost, unless
"The substance of things hoped for" is truth. . . .

Then this smiling at each new messenger,
Pale as Jocasta, would not be death

But life. Meanwhile
Must speak "as under correction."
"These things are a great mystery."
Human. Liable to self-deception.

For the Spirit that can stir the village dust
Moves him to no godlike gesture. He is less
A sacred relic than a reconciler. No Colonnus
Beckons with confirming thunder.

PENELOPE

PENELOPE

A Theater Lyric

Characters

ODYSSEUS
PENELOPE
TELEMACHUS
EUMAEUS, *an old man, Odysseus' swineherd and sheepherder*
EURYCLEIA ⎱ *middle-aged women, loyal to Penelope*
EURYNOME ⎰

Penelope's Wooers:
   ANTINOUS
   AMPHINOMUS
   EURYMACHUS
   and several others, young men only slightly older than Telemachus
Several womenservants, now lovers of the wooers

THE PROPERTY MAN ⎱ *who present and explain the*
THE MUSICIAN ⎰ *show*

The scene is Odysseus' farm in Ithaca, and the time the day and the night of his return.

> (*The curtain rises in silence. The stage looks empty, as though the set had not yet been put up. A few flats are folded against each side wall. EUMAEUS—old, a peasant—is standing quietly with his back to the audience, peering upstage. The stage space, with the walls and fly gallery visible, is dimly and coolly lighted, as though shortly before sunrise.*)

MUSICIAN
(*Calling offstage.*) All ready, props?
   (*He enters.*)

45

Property Man

(*Coming to meet him.*) All ready. The stage is empty for the prologue. (*To audience.*) We're down on the beach near Eumaeus' hut, at the edge of Odysseus' farm.

Musician

When I blow the horn Odysseus is to come from the sea—you know, the "winedark sea." Many, many years since he went away to war. . . . Now we are getting ready to show you his return, and the crucial day.

Props

Blow. Sound your horn.

(Musician *blows a call on his horn.*)

Props

(*To audience.*) Patient Odysseus: ten years of war, ten years of wandering without a name, with nothing his own. Yet he wouldn't believe Calypso on her ocean island. He wouldn't yield to the sirens with their sweet song. He wouldn't eat the Oxen of the Sun but, fearing the god, departed hungry. When the Cyclops shouted, WHAT SHALL I CALL YOU? he called back, NO MAN!

(Musician *blows the call again.*)

(Odysseus *appears upstage as a tattered beggar leaning on a staff. He comes slowly down, peering from side to side as though weary from a long journey.*)

Props

Saving his passion. Patient; dangerous:

MUSICIAN

Remembering Penelope, Telemachus, and his own land.

ODYSSEUS

(*Seeing* EUMAEUS, *whom we now make out down-stage in the shadow.*) Tell me, friend, what country or what island have I reached?

EUMAEUS

This is Ithaca, stranger.

ODYSSEUS

Ah.

EUMAEUS

It's narrow and rocky, but a good country for men and for sheep, they used to say.

ODYSSEUS

As you see, I am a beggar. Starving.

EUMAEUS

I don't have much these days.

ODYSSEUS

(*Looking off.*) And if I go up to the house?

EUMAEUS

Don't go.

ODYSSEUS

No hospitality there, for a stranger?

EUMAEUS

Not any more. Not since Odysseus went away to war. His wife, Penelope, sees no one now. His son

47

Telemachus can hardly feed himself, much less you.
The men I work for now are in the house all day with
their drinking and singing: Penelope's wooers. They
don't like beggars. If you ask them for help, who
knows what the end would be? Better go back to the
sea.

(*Pause.*)

ODYSSEUS

The sun is coming up behind Mount Neriton. And
now I smell again the freshness of the fields. . . . But
this is only in the mind, a trick of memory to deceive
me. I am still at sea.

EUMAEUS

Eh? . . . Who are you?

ODYSSEUS

You can't tell at all, Eumaeus?

EUMAEUS

(*Peering.*) I'm an old man. I remember things the
others have forgotten. Looking at you, now, it's as if
it were Odysseus I was seeing!

ODYSSEUS

(*Straightens up so that his rags fall back; takes*
EUMAEUS' *hand.*) Ah, Eumaeus.

EUMAEUS

Oh . . . Oh!

ODYSSEUS

Don't grieve. This is a *good* omen—that you, at
least, are the same.

EUMAEUS

You're *here?* Since when? By what ship did you come? Alone—like this?

ODYSSEUS

Just as you see me, Eumaeus. For the rest—I hope I can tell you everything in time. But now—there would be too much to tell you now, Eumaeus. . . . You say my house is dangerous, now, even for a beggar.

EUMAEUS

Yes.

ODYSSEUS

Am I too late?

EUMAEUS

Twenty years is a long time. Out of sight, out of mind.

ODYSSEUS

(*After a pause.*) Listen, Eumaeus. Of the men who were trying to get back home when that war was over—Agamemnon, Menelaus, Nestor—many others I knew—some were lost in the Ocean. Some reached home, but found in their bed, left cold too long, a fatal snare, their longings wrong. Yet some there were who found what was better than they deserved or had a right to expect. . . . What shall I find, Eumaeus?

EUMAEUS

What can I say?

49

ODYSSEUS

You must tell me what you know. How is it with Penelope? Do you know? Who are the men in my house—her wooers, you say?

EUMAEUS

Antinous. Eurymachus. Amphinomus. Men from Hylos and Zacynthus.

ODYSSEUS

Craving another man's wife?

EUMAEUS

And his living. His life, you might say—the way they eat up the house. It's three years now, since they began coming—like dogs, from miles around—as they got to know about the woman, and no man with her.

ODYSSEUS

Aaa!

EUMAEUS

And Telemachus—almost a man now. Growing up. But only to learn, more and more, what he missed. And as he gets his strength the men begin to think he's dangerous. He's just back from a journey he took, looking for you. The boy couldn't think of anything else to try. Some of the men waited for him by the Headland of Zacynthus, to get him on his way back, put him out of the way. But he passed there at night, and they missed him.

ODYSSEUS

Aaa!

EUMAEUS

They won't hurt him here at the farm, where
people could see. But he—but I don't think he can
last long.

(*Pause.*)

ODYSSEUS

(*Softly.*) And Penelope? What have they done to
her—who lived, when I knew her, for one thing
only?

EUMAEUS

I don't know. She used to say Odysseus was still a
living man, though she couldn't tell where. But she
can't keep time from going. And everyone can see
that time gives her the lie. She can't keep the men
from eating up her house that's never repaired—nor
keep Telemachus from growing and feeling the needs
of a man inside him. Lately she says nothing. I don't
see her. The two women, Eurycleia and Eurynome
are with her.

> (*Pause.* ODYSSEUS *slowly stoops back into his
> beggar's posture, pulling the gray hair down
> over his eyes.*)

EUMAEUS

What are you doing?

ODYSSEUS

Tell no one you saw me. Forget it yourself.

EUMAEUS

Back to the sea again—leaving us?

51

ODYSSEUS

No, Eumaeus.

EUMAEUS

You don't want me to get word to Penelope, if I can? Or Telemachus?

ODYSSEUS

Only that a strange beggar is about the farm.

EUMAEUS

Then you . . .

ODYSSEUS

I'm going to the evening meal in the house. I must see for myself.

EUMAEUS

There are many of them. Sure of themselves. Strong and dangerous.

ODYSSEUS

It's not *that* I'm afraid of.

EUMAEUS

Eh?

ODYSSEUS

But a certain cold illness about the heart. What have I lost? An exile is a bodiless ghost. And now I know that when he revisits his native earth, the life that has his place is poison to him—a second sentence of death.

EUMAEUS

. . . Who can tell? What's coming will come soon, if you go up there with them.

ODYSSEUS

Let it come.

EUMAEUS

I am with you.

ODYSSEUS

Then pray to the gods to give me patience, Eumaeus. While I learn, bit by bit, what's there in the house, and what it is I have to do.

(MUSICIAN *blows his horn again.* ODYSSEUS *goes off, intent, leaning on his staff.* EUMAEUS *watches him go, then disappears in the other direction. The stage is empty again except for* PROPS *and* MUSICIAN.)

PROPS AND MUSICIAN

(*To audience.*) The little sail passes the headland toward the open ocean, fades to a speck, is lost to sight.

Silence. Spring; Summer; Autumn; Winter. None to see. None to hear.

Hope coming in silence, and going again with the long swells of the sea.

Does this silence give permission for the spirit's death?

Slow stealth of lust? Swift stealth of murder?

Summer. Autumn. Winter.

53

Spring: in the oblivion of the warm rains, the mindless growing of the grass.

In the abyss of time, mortals moving; on the sea, on the earth.

> (*The twanging of a stringed instrument is faintly heard offstage.*)

PROPS

(*Going upstage.*) Come. The men are waiting. Time to mark out their place.

> (PROPS *and* MUSICIAN *unfold the flats which were leaning at the sides of the stage. They represent a thick plastered wall, with narrow dark slits for windows, and in the center big heavy doors studded with iron, which can be used. The courtyard of a farmhouse in a Mediterranean country is suggested—the blank, sunbaked façade. which changes little with the centuries. It occupies the center of the stage, but we are aware of the undressed stage above and around it.*)

MUSICIAN

(*Explaining as they work.*) The sunny wall with the big doors.

PROPS

Benches, where they loaf. Put them in a kind of ring. For their sports. And sometimes their fights.

MUSICIAN

Bring up the lights. (PROPS *does so.*) (*To audience.*) Late afternoon. The house is set on a hill, with a view of the sea. Imagine dust, the smell of sweat and leather.

PROPS

No Penelope. But Telemachus is to be drawn into their ring, as a fly to poisoned honey. Fatherless Telemachus! And the struggle starts again. (*To* MUSICIAN.) Come.

(*As the set was sketched out the twanging grew louder, and now as* PROPS *and* MUSICIAN *come down to the sides of the proscenium, the suitors begin drifting in. They are handsome young men; their costume suggests that of a modern peasantry. Two of them are fencers.*)

FIRST FENCER

See—like this . . . and this . . . then *this*.

SECOND FENCER

Let's try it.

(*They fence.*)

AMPHINOMUS

(*Enters, singing as he strums.*)

A woman is weak, a woman is strong
As the delicate webs of her veils—
Webs of pain, webs of joy
That bind a man till he have his way.

Iron promises never fulfilled,
Those delicate, bewildering webs—
Meshes of pain and joy in the mind
That torment a man till he have his way;

That weaken and torment a man
Till he have his way.

(*During the end of the song* TELEMACHUS
*enters and stands—thin, poorly dressed, tense, at
the edge of their circle.*)

EURYMACHUS

Look.

ANTINOUS

Don't be afraid. The men won't hurt you.

(*Laughter.*)

TELEMACHUS

Why should I be afraid of my guests?

AMPHINOMUS

He's going to be stiff with us.

ANTINOUS

(*After pause.*) You didn't find your father?

TELEMACHUS

No.

ANTINOUS

Never mind. We'll take care of you. You need a
new coat, I see.

AMPHINOMUS

And a drink.

TELEMACHUS

At my expense.

(*Pause.* AMPHINOMUS *strums lightly.*)

56

EURYMACHUS

Well, did you think things over on your journey?
What are you going to do about Penelope? It's time
you were a man, Telemachus, high time.

ANTINOUS

Come tonight. I'll have Eurymachus, here, find a
woman for you.

(*Titters.*)

TELEMACHUS

Thanks. I see you've been planning for me while I
was away. Pleasure behind the stairs . . . and death
out by Zacynthus, where no one could hear a cry or a
splash.

(*Silent pause.*)

EURYMACHUS

If the puppy repeats that in the village there'll be
trouble.

ANTINOUS

Who would care, any more? The village is bored
with his gloomy face.

TELEMACHUS

Do you really think so? Then kill me now, eh?

ANTINOUS

Have patience.

(*Pause; strumming.*)

AMPHINOMUS

Listen, Telemachus, it's your mother who taught
you that we aren't good enough for you. It's Penel-

ope who holds you like a fool here, in her nets. Tell
him, Antinous.

ANTINOUS

Mm—you *should* be old enough now, to understand this . . . When we first came, asking Penelope
to take one of us, she told us she had to weave a
shroud for old Laertes first. That stopped us. We
believed she was pious.

TELEMACHUS

She told you she was waiting for Odysseus! It was
when you wouldn't believe in *him* that she began her
shroud!

(*Laughter.*)

ANTINOUS

Listen: day after day she would be weaving, and
couldn't speak to us.

AMPHINOMUS

We could feast our eyes, but nothing else.

ANTINOUS

And night after night, behind closed doors, she
unraveled that shroud she pretended she was weaving
—unraveled everything, Telemachus.

TELEMACHUS

I know all that.

ANTINOUS

But this is the point: a woman can bewilder and
destroy a man, if she gives him nothing he needs, puts

him off and puts him off. No satisfaction in that. . . .
Look at you.

AMPHINOMUS

I think he sees. . . . You're neither boy nor man,
while she holds *us*. Go sit by Penelope. Tell her her
son is a sort of stray dog around the house. Tell her
she must give up and leave you some place you can
call yours.

TELEMACHUS

(*In pain and anger.*) Aaaa!

EURYMACHUS

Tell her at once.

TELEMACHUS

Turn her out of her own house!

ANTINOUS

She can't hide much longer.

TELEMACHUS

(*To himself.*) Her house a barracks. (*To them.*)
You've planned well! Her maids filching her pretty
things—giggling as they sneak off with you behind
her back!

(*Laughter.*)

ANTINOUS

That's her cue. I can tell by her voice.

EURYMACHUS

By her veils.

AMPHINOMUS

By her eyes.

ANTINOUS

By the scent she uses.

TELEMACHUS

She's waiting for Odysseus!

(*Laughter.*)

You're in another man's house! When he comes . . .

(*Laughter, which quiets as they eye him. Strumming again.*)

ANTINOUS

You're a little hysterical, Telemachus. Remember, we are your guests.

TELEMACHUS

(*Getting control.*) Thank you for reminding me. I turn no man from my doors: I can last—with this twiddling music forever in my ears!

(*Enter, slowly,* EUMAEUS.)

EURYMACHUS

Another skull at the feast.

ANTINOUS

Are they getting a good meal ready for us?

EUMAEUS

Yes. Better than you think.

MEN

Ah.

(*They get up lazily, one or two drift into the house.*)

ANTINOUS

Plenty of wine?

EUMAEUS

Yes. And torches for tonight.

AMPHINOMUS

We'll drink to mysterious Penelope!
(*Goes.*)

ANTINOUS

(*Going.*) Mysterious to Telemachus.
(*Laughter. The men have gone into the house; the doors are closed and the music fades out.* TELEMACHUS *and* EUMAEUS *are left alone.*)

TELEMACHUS

(*Slowly.*) Why did I ever think I could find my father—beyond the Ocean? And when I failed, what was it that drew me back?

EUMAEUS

(*Peering at him.*) Some things are beyond our strength. . . . What are you thinking?

TELEMACHUS

I told them this would go on forever, this empty waiting. As though nothing had changed. But they know better. And I can tell *you*, Eumaeus; *not long*. I'm beginning to see what I have to do.

EUMAEUS

What's that?

TELEMACHUS

I'm beginning to understand clearly. When I saw my mother this morning she told me she'd had a dream that she can't get out of her mind.

EUMAEUS

Penelope? What did she dream?

TELEMACHUS

She wouldn't tell me. But now, after what they said, I can guess. Her dreams always mean one thing: her feeling is changing, she's coming to a decision. . . . You see, while I was a child, she could postpone everything—till Odysseus returned, she used to say —till I grew strong enough to act myself. But now I've failed to find Odysseus. And now it's dawned on her that I'm grown already, and still helpless. She thinks the time has come for her to go off with one of them, and leave me the house. She would do it, Eumaeus, and tell me nothing! Mother, mother. . . . Thinking she'd help me. Everything hers, even my life. . . . But the men are right. The end is very close.

EUMAEUS

The men are wrong. And you don't know what she dreamed, what she's deciding.

TELEMACHUS

I see what pulled me back. This country, the hills,
the sheep; like an animal haunting its native earth.
Like a child, thinking the familiar things—those trees,
the house—would always last. But now I see them in
a new light: they betrayed me: and while I linger
here in a kind of homesickness my mother's wooers
feed on me, peck me to death—like the healthy fowls
in the barnyard when they find one sick! Aaaaaa!
Even mother can no longer ask me to submit to that.

EUMAEUS

(*After a pause.*) What can you do?

TELEMACHUS

Bring it to the test.

EUMAEUS

They are much stronger than you.

TELEMACHUS

And yet, if I wait for them tonight, behind the
house, as they come out one by one, drunk after their
feast—I could spring from behind in the dark, plant
a knife in the nape of the neck—I could take two or
three of them with me under the dust.

EUMAEUS

And toss away all hope? (*Shaking his head.*) Too
young, too young for that.

TELEMACHUS

I think it's the will of the gods, for the beasts and
for us. This only seems a human house: underneath

it's a foxes' thicket. I'm willing. I need it, need to
strike at last, like any creature cornered.

EUMAEUS

Leave that to them. No man needs death.

TELEMACHUS

Not they, perhaps.

EUMAEUS

And yet . . . if help came. . . . Help that you
can't see . . . closer than you think . . .

TELEMACHUS

Help?

EUMAEUS

Then nothing would be lost.

TELEMACHUS

(*After looking closely at him.*) I think you have
something you want to tell me. I can't make out
whether it's good or bad. What is it, Eumaeus? Tell
me.

EUMAEUS

What I can. That's why I'm here.

TELEMACHUS

What, *what*, Eumaeus?

EUMAEUS

Patience. Not much.

TELEMACHUS

Only one thing would help me: it's weak to count,
now, on that.

EUMAEUS

What?

TELEMACHUS

My father.

EUMAEUS

(*After pause.*) Yes . . .

TELEMACHUS

I don't believe you.

EUMAEUS

Believe what? But I can tell you this: a stranger, a
beggar, has appeared at the farm. He's asking for *you*.

TELEMACHUS

For *me?*

EUMAEUS

For Telemachus, he says. The son of Odysseus.

TELEMACHUS

For *me?* What can he want?

EUMAEUS

That *you* must find out. I've told you all I could.

TELEMACHUS

Who is he?

65

EUMAEUS

He doesn't say.

TELEMACHUS

Where is he now?

EUMAEUS

I don't know. But he will come to the evening meal in the house. You must be host again. He's counting on *you*.

TELEMACHUS

(*After pause.*) On a scarecrow host. A rag doll— that the men handle as they wish. . . . Must I really go back, Eumaeus—take up that fight again with shadows?

EUMAEUS

(*Nodding.*) And watch. In patience.

TELEMACHUS

(*Turns slowly toward the house, then back to* EUMAEUS.) Can you tell me nothing else?

EUMAEUS

What could it be? . . . Since you are young, and your life is before you, I might tell you this: we don't earn all we get. For sometimes, beyond our strength, in ways we couldn't see or expect—closer than we think, help comes to meet us.

(TELEMACHUS *turns his face slowly toward the house, walks toward it, opens the door with a burst of music and laughter from inside, goes in, closing the door after him. Silence. The door sud-*

66

denly opens again and over the music ANTINOUS
calls.)

ANTINOUS

Eumaeus! Eumaeus! Are you dreaming?

EUMAEUS

Perhaps.

ANTINOUS

More wine! Wine for Telemachus' guests!

EUMAEUS

(*Going in.*) So—you're reaching your pitch.

(*Doors close. Silence. The stage in semidarkness.* PROPS *and* MUSICIAN, *left alone, speak to audience.*)

PROPS AND MUSICIAN

The light has long since lifted from the tops of the trees and the upper windows of the farmhouse.

While Penelope, unseen, two women with her, still suffers her dreams: rumors of the end. What is she in herself?

The men are burning torches, keeping the night out, burning torches till she declare herself.

(*Pause.*)

The chickens have settled to rest on their dark roosts, content that the day end, and their eyes close;

But the humans, hoping always against hope, can't stop—brightly urging their murderous faces upon each other, upon the dark,

Feeling, denying, that their time is short.

Open the doors on that Masque.

(Tables, benches, and torches have been set up behind the façade of the house, to suggest a big room; and when the doors are folded back, this scene is revealed, bright in the surrounding darkness of the stage space. Music, laughter. The men are eating and drinking, and some dancing in the edges of the lighted space. Six or eight women, "the perjured maids," are busy serving food and wine. TELEMACHUS, as host, sits solitary near the center. After a moment ODYSSEUS appears downstage silhouetted against the light, his back to the audience, watching the feast. He advances slowly, leaning on his staff, acting the old beggar. The men gradually become aware of him, and begin to watch. The music quiets to a throb.)

ANTINOUS

(To TELEMACHUS.*)* Now what's *this?*

TELEMACHUS

(For answer, fills a bowl with food and sends it by one of the women to ODYSSEUS.*)* You are at home here, stranger.

ODYSSEUS

A good word.

(Sits on doorstep, eats and watches.)

ANTINOUS

You're going to let him feed here? Look: the old belly under the rags is greedy as death! *(Titters.)*

68

TELEMACHUS

(*Tense.*) Stranger, ask the men for whatever you wish.

(ODYSSEUS *slowly gets up and approaches* ANTINOUS *with his bowl.*)

ANTINOUS

What do you want?

ODYSSEUS

Penelope's feast.

ANTINOUS

Brazen, eh? Stand back, and hush.

(ODYSSEUS *withdraws.*)

EURYMACHUS

He's old, but his eye is poisonous.

ANTINOUS

And his mouth. We'll shut it.

(ANTINOUS *suddenly throws a stool at* ODYSSEUS, *which hits his shoulder and clatters to the floor. The women scream and run out, the men jump up.*)

TELEMACHUS

(*With knife.*) He is my guest!

(*Loud laughter.*)

ODYSSEUS

(*Going back to the door, shaking his head.*) Take what the gods send tonight. (*Sits. Men quiet.*)

Though there's no joy in a beating for the belly's sake.
(*Eats.*)

TELEMACHUS

Oh. Oh.

AMPHINOMUS

(*Getting drunk.*) Don't.

EURYMACHUS

(*To* ANTINOUS.) Do we know where he came
from? What mischief he might start?

ANTINOUS

He's harmless—except for that prying voice. Let
him hush.

AMPHINOMUS

Does he know what the gods want? Give me a
drink!

MEN

(*Laughing.*) A drink, a drink!

TELEMACHUS

(*Yelling.*) Wine! Wine for my guests!

(*The men go upstage, the women flood back,
and the revel starts again.* TELEMACHUS *is left
downstage staring at* ODYSSEUS.)

TELEMACHUS

Who are you?

ODYSSEUS

Hush.

TELEMACHUS

You've put me to shame.

ODYSSEUS

The shame is mine.

TELEMACHUS

. . . What?

ODYSSEUS

Hush, Telemachus. (*Points behind him.*) Hush!

(AMPHINOMUS *emerges from the crowd.*)

AMPHINOMUS

I want to know what the gods send tonight!

ANTINOUS

He's drunk.

(*Music has quieted to a throb; tittering crowd
gathers to watch.*)

AMPHINOMUS

(*Crouching by* ODYSSEUS.) Telemachus is right,
you're at home here—stay!

EURYMACHUS

He's going to cry. Everybody must love him when
he's drunk.

ANTINOUS

Penelope too?

(*Laughter.*)

ODYSSEUS

(*Slowly, to* AMPHINOMUS.) Do you say so?

AMPHINOMUS

But tell me if you know—what do the gods want?

ODYSSEUS

Then I'll tell you: get out. Move fast while it's dark. Never come back.

AMPHINOMUS

. . . What!

ANTINOUS

You asked for it.

ODYSSEUS

These are not your friends, they only seem so. This is not your house. Penelope doesn't love you. The night and the wine won't last. Get out tonight.

ANTINOUS

(*To* AMPHINOMUS.) Startled, eh? Stumbled over a carcass?

(*Laughs.*)

AMPHINOMUS

Who is this?

ANTINOUS

An old windbag. Dreary, eh? You did it! *You* waked that voice!

AMPHINOMUS

A lying voice!

(*Throws wine in* ODYSSEUS' *face.*)

The night is young!

(*Loud laughter.*)

72

ANTINOUS

Good old Amphinomus! Drink this! And this!

(*They rush him upstage reeling, and the revel starts again at a higher pitch than before.*)

TELEMACHUS

(*Down with* ODYSSEUS.) You?

ODYSSEUS

Yes, Telemachus.

TELEMACHUS

Like this, in *your house?*

ODYSSEUS

Sh, they'd kill us both.

TELEMACHUS

This is a nightmare!

ODYSSEUS

Yes—go back, be host.

TELEMACHUS

How long?

ODYSSEUS

I will try to make it short.

TELEMACHUS

Are they blind?

ODYSSEUS

Yes. Hold fast.

(TELEMACHUS *pauses for one more look at his father, rushes back into the throng.*)

73

TELEMACHUS

Wine! More wine for my guests!

(*The revel still mounts. Presently* ODYSSEUS *creeps forward on his hands and knees, and seizes one of the women as she hurries past with a jug of wine.*)

ODYSSEUS

Penelope is alone.

MAID

Yes!

ODYSSEUS

Run to your mistress and beg her pardon.

MAID

Not I. Let me go!

ODYSSEUS

I'll serve in your place.

MAID

Do you think that's why I stay?

ODYSSEUS

No.

MAID

Who are you, old man? You've lost your wits!

ODYSSEUS

(*Pulls her sharply to her knees.*) It's you who are lost.

(*She screams, drops the jug and runs out.*)

ANTINOUS

(*Over the din.*) What's this? What's this?

> (ODYSSEUS *picks up the jug, and slowly proceeds to fill cups. The music a-throb again, as the revelers turn from their interrupted drinks and embraces to watch.*)

ANTINOUS

The old man again—what's he up to now?

AMPHINOMUS

Is he eternal?

EURYMACHUS

Look: he's been creeping in with the women. Do you want a skirt, father?

ODYSSEUS

The fool's eye mirrors itself; you see only wantonness. But look!

> (*Starts carefully drawing a ring on the floor with a trickle of wine from his jug.*)

ANTINOUS

Crazed with age. And envy of us.

ODYSSEUS

(*Suddenly drops the jug and crouches in a fighter's posture at edge of circle; to* EURYMACHUS.) A knife! A knife for each of us!

EURYMACHUS

What!

> (*Reaches for a knife and throws it at* ODYSSEUS, *who dodges. The knife hits one of the men, he*

lunges at EURYMACHUS, *and a fight starts.*
Women scream and flock out again. Furniture
overturned; confusion.)

ANTINOUS

(*Drunk.*) Stop. (*Separates the fighters; silence; the*
women flock back to watch.) You're fools.

AMPHINOMUS

What's come over us since *he* was in the house?

(*Sobs.*)

TELEMACHUS

And mastered you! Your eyes are glassy as beasts'!
Go home! You've drunk too much! The feast is over!

ANTINOUS

More over than he thinks—the feast he never en-
joyed.

(*He takes one of the women and pulls her to*
him. Other men do likewise. The women begin
to giggle, also the men, eyeing TELEMACHUS.)

TELEMACHUS

Can't you *hear!* Laughter like crying! Meaningless!

AMPHINOMUS

Crying for Telemachus!

(AMPHINOMUS, *drunk, starts again a spas-*
modic strumming; the couples, laughing, glanc-
ing over their shoulders at TELEMACHUS, *begin*
drifting off. They take most of the torches with
them.)

76

TELEMACHUS

(*As they disappear.*) Are you dreaming? Answer
me!

> (*He is left alone, the stage dim, the laughter
> and now and then the strumming, going away
> offstage.*)

TELEMACHUS

(*Staring about him.*) Or am I . . . ? (*He sees* ODYS-
SEUS *in the shadow.*) You are my father?

ODYSSEUS

(*Softly.*) Yes, Telemachus.

TELEMACHUS

(*Lost.*) Ah . . .

ODYSSEUS

(*Stands up to his full height, crosses to* TELEMA-
CHUS *and takes his hand.*) The truth is always smaller
than you think.

TELEMACHUS

My father . . . I was right? Not dreaming? And
they were wrong?

ODYSSEUS

You can be sure no other Odysseus will ever come,
Telemachus, to his own wife and his own son.

TELEMACHUS

(*Melted.*) Odysseus.

77

ODYSSEUS

You're a little shaken, and no wonder.

(*Distant strumming. Both listen. It stops.*)

TELEMACHUS

Blind they are!

ODYSSEUS

Blind and dangerous.

TELEMACHUS

But you *came*. . . . How did you come?

ODYSSEUS

On a Phaeacian ship; I want to tell you, Telemachus, but now . . .

(*They listen. Strumming, farther away, starts and stops.*)

TELEMACHUS

They could kill you.

ODYSSEUS

Sh. . . . We must think. We have a little time now.

TELEMACHUS

Why did you risk it—risk everything—like *this?*

ODYSSEUS

No choice. I must see my way.

TELEMACHUS

What the gods wish?

78

ODYSSEUS

That we must guess.

(*Both listen—far off strumming, then silence.*)

TELEMACHUS

What will *they* do next?

ODYSSEUS

Sleep, I think—their night is dying down. But not well, and not long. . . . And when they wake . . .

TELEMACHUS

What then?

ODYSSEUS

I'm afraid they'll be decided. How can they draw back—how can they rest till they do what they somehow failed to do last night?

TELEMACHUS

Then we must hurry, we must arm! I'll get Eumaeus. When they see *how* they failed—that the beggar was Odysseus!

ODYSSEUS

(*Shaking his head.*) Not yet.

TELEMACHUS

Don't you want to punish them, father, show them that you are alive, master of this house?

ODYSSEUS

Yes. But I'm not. And I mustn't yield them our one weapon, few as we are, you and I and Eumaeus.

TELEMACHUS

What weapon?

ODYSSEUS

Their stubborn blindness. By *that*, if at all, they'll be
lost. . . . Unless *I'm* lost.

TELEMACHUS

You, father?

ODYSSEUS

I can't find, in the house or about the farm, a trace
of Penelope.

TELEMACHUS

Penelope?

ODYSSEUS

Where is she, Telemachus?

TELEMACHUS

In the south wing of the house.

ODYSSEUS

Alone?

TELEMACHUS

Eurycleia and Eurynome are with her.

ODYSSEUS

If I could see her without betraying too much. . . .
You trust no one in the house?

TELEMACHUS

Those who aren't false might lose their heads.

80

ODYSSEUS

It's as if she didn't exist—the Penelope I thought I knew. Here, in the gutted house she used to keep so neat—only her name to remind me of her, when the lewd men take it on their lips. Mistrust, guilt, desolation all about her.

TELEMACHUS

And now I'm afraid she won't leave us much time. I think she's about to do something herself.

ODYSSEUS

What's that?

TELEMACHUS

She wouldn't tell me.

ODYSSEUS

Why?

TELEMACHUS

They think they've got her.

ODYSSEUS

Do you?

TELEMACHUS

While she waits, she thinks, they have my place and I am lost. She feels trapped. They count on that.

ODYSSEUS

Aaa!

TELEMACHUS

We must get them, father!

ODYSSEUS

How?

TELEMACHUS

Now—before they wake!

ODYSSEUS

Like desperate rats? While Penelope, also in the
dark . . . *You* don't trust her either, Telemachus?

TELEMACHUS

(*After a pause.*) It's you she needs.

ODYSSEUS

Aaaa!

TELEMACHUS

And now—while we wait for her—we lose our
chance!

ODYSSEUS

(*After a pause.*) I begin to see what it's been, waiting, seeing nothing! Nothing but *them*. . . . Ah,
Telemachus. But you must hold a little longer. The
pull of *their* impatience gets stronger and faster—but
we are lost if we think too much of them. Like staring
into a millrace. Now we must draw back.

TELEMACHUS

We *must*, father?

ODYSSEUS

Till the whole shape of the evil, where it spreds
through the house, reveal itself, if it will. Even though
it show everything empty and false! . . . We have

done what we can. We must try to quiet our disappointment. (*Listens.*) They too are quiet. . . . We must try to rest.

TELEMACHUS

With danger all about us?

ODYSSEUS

Yes. As if the ocean were under us.

TELEMACHUS

You are with me.

ODYSSEUS

I thank the gods for that, Telemachus! Come. I will tell you about the tireless Proteus.

TELEMACHUS

(*Coming.*) Proteus, father? What's he?

(*They sit side by side, looking out before them.*)

ODYSSEUS

The Old Man of the Sea. You should be warned of *him!* It's when you're stranded on some empty shore that he first comes, Telemachus, especially if you're young—he prefers the young for his prey. He's on your back and strangling you before you know it. And then, if you lose heart, you must do his will. If you turn and try to grip him he changes shape. A lion. A deer. A lightning snake—then soft, perhaps, to fool you, like some pathetic sea-thing.

TELEMACHUS

What can you do?

83

ODYSSEUS

Never kill him.

TELEMACHUS

Never, father?

ODYSSEUS

Yet if you could hang on, they say, to every beast shape, guilt or fear—however he whines or you cry with pain—he would grow quiet, they say, and when you're quiet, tell you the truth at last. For he knows the future, what's coming for you.

TELEMACHUS

Whether evil or good?

ODYSSEUS

So they say . . .

(ODYSSEUS *and* TELEMACHUS *look out before them, alert, quiet, waiting.*)

PROPS AND MUSICIAN

(*Softly to audience.*) Imagine, beyond the highest treetops of the farm, the slow revolution of the stars;

Beyond our power the slow night goes.

Though with that vast shifting,

Lifting, filling the passionate human,

Knowledge comes, too late to change, of what is done,

Of what is lost or found.

(*Pause. Slight noise offstage. Both* ODYSSEUS *and* TELEMACHUS *hear it.*)

TELEMACHUS

(*In whisper, slowly standing up.*) Too late.

ODYSSEUS

(*Concealing a knife under his rags, crouches slowly back into his beggar posture in the shadows.*) You do not know me.

(*Pause. Enter EURYCLEIA.*)

TELEMACHUS

Eurycleia! . . . What is it?

EURYCLEIA

I have a message for the stranger from Penelope.

TELEMACHUS

From Penelope? . . . The stranger is there.

EURYCLEIA

Penelope has heard that you were here, and have been treated badly. She can't prevent it, she says, or make amends—but she asked me to tell you that she won't let you go away hungry.

ODYSSEUS

(*Moved.*) Thank her for me.

EURYCLEIA

In return, she asks an odd favor from you.

ODYSSEUS

Whatever she asks me.

EURYCLEIA

She had a dream last night which won't let her rest, for she thinks it's trying to tell her something. But

dreams, she says, have two gates they come
through: the gates of ivory and the gates of horn.
Those that come through the gates of horn are true,
but those that come through the gates of ivory deceive us. Somehow she thinks that *you* could tell her
whether the dream she had is false or true.

ODYSSEUS

What did she dream?

EURYCLEIA

Twenty white geese she has, that she feeds every
morning by her window—she treasures them. But she
dreamed that an eagle swooped down from Mount
Neriton and killed them. There they lay—their pretty
necks all broken and awry. She cried in her dream;
but then, it seemed, the eagle was back, and he told
her that the geese were her wooers and he Odysseus come back to save her. When she awoke, she
was laughing—yet crying still.

(*Pause.*)

ODYSSEUS

(*Softly.*) Tell Penelope it was a good dream,
and true.

EURYCLEIA

Thank you, stranger. That's wise. Now, perhaps,
she can rest.

(*She goes out.*)

TELEMACHUS

(*Awed.*) Father—what does she know?

86

ODYSSEUS

Everything, and nothing.

TELEMACHUS

Who you are?

ODYSSEUS

She may guess, she may hope, yet not dare to admit it even to herself.

TELEMACHUS

But her dream—was it really a good sign, father? Even for *us?*

ODYSSEUS

The best. The spirit that first brought her to this house is alive, Telemachus! In her tender dream I recognize it. Thank the gods.

TELEMACHUS

Then . . .

ODYSSEUS

Hush.

(*Sob offstage.* ODYSSEUS *shrinks back.*)

TELEMACHUS

It's Eurycleia, back again. She's crying.

(*Enter* EURYCLEIA.)

EURYCLEIA

Penelope says, sleep here, tonight, by the fire, stranger.

87

ODYSSEUS

She says that?

EURYCLEIA

For tomorrow, she says, the fate of the house will be decided and she may no longer be here herself.

TELEMACHUS

What did she mean, Eurycleia?

EURYCLEIA

She doesn't say. She's packing. Putting her things away as after a funeral in the house.

TELEMACHUS

What is she going to do?

EURYCLEIA

I can't tell. I only know I'm to fetch the key to the arms cupboard that hasn't been opened since your father went away. She's coming herself to open it and bring out something she says she needs today.

(*Exit* EURYCLEIA.)

TELEMACHUS

What I feared the most.

ODYSSEUS

It's here, Telemachus.

TELEMACHUS

More than what the men could do to us.

ODYSSEUS

She is more deeply hurt.

TELEMACHUS

First turning toward you, then away. Against nature! Taking your weapons! A woman is so awk-
ward, father—and we, as though we didn't exist, must
wait here helpless!

ODYSSEUS

She's cutting to the quick. Come. Help her.

TELEMACHUS

What will she do?

ODYSSEUS

What she can't tell them, or us, or even herself.
The spirit within her craves to make answer, and we
too must want it. She will bring forth something
long overdue to speak for her; we must make it
answer for all of us . . . I think the weapon she
wants is not for her, but for them and for us.

TELEMACHUS

Then . . . she can't prevent the fight, father?

ODYSSEUS

Or the slaughter. . . . Collect all the knives and
spears. Get them out of sight.

TELEMACHUS

(*Short sigh.*) At last.

(*Moves with eager stealth to get the weapons together.*)

ODYSSEUS

Lock them up at the end of the hall.

89

TELEMACHUS

Then we can strike! . . . But *you*, father?

ODYSSEUS

While I watch.

TELEMACHUS

Still crouched? As a stranger in your house? An empty beggar?

ODYSSEUS

Since that is her wish.

(TELEMACHUS *goes off in silence with the weapons.* ODYSSEUS *shrinks slowly into himself. We hear a sob offstage, then* EURYCLEIA's *voice.*)

EURYCLEIA

(*Whispering.*) Pull yourself together.

(EURYCLEIA *and* EURYNOME *move steadily across the stage, with set faces.* EURYCLEIA *is carrying a big key;* EURYNOME *follows her with several folds of cloths and napkins over her arm.*)

PROPS

The women prepare their mystery. The mystery of Penelope's hour come upon her . . .

(PENELOPE *appears, a long soft scarf over her head and shoulders. She has the big key. She crosses the stage softly and steadily, looking neither to right nor left, the two women following her.* ODYSSEUS, *watching, makes no sign.*)

MUSICIAN

(*Continuing.*) The unwished burden within her; hope against hope; now ripe at last . . .

PROPS

Soon, now, to trouble her no longer.

(*The women have disappeared. Brief pause.*)

She won't fail now. Willing, unseeing, willing . . .

MUSICIAN

. . . that what they did to her come forth. Whether death or a new life.

(PENELOPE *appears, returning at the same steady, rapt pace. She is clumsily carrying a huge bow, and under her arm a number of arrows. Behind her come the two women, one after the other, lugging between them twelve battle-axes.*)

PROPS

She walks by faith.

MUSICIAN

Closed, till then:

PROPS

Till the issue speaks for her.

(*The women have disappeared.* TELEMACHUS *is back, upstage.*)

TELEMACHUS

The weapons are safe. Did you see what she did?

ODYSSEUS

Yes . . . Now we must make ready: Fasten every
window . . . Close the doors.

(TELEMACHUS *softly closes the big doors. On
the stage there is a little more cool light.*)

PROPS

The dark is nearly spent. A chilly breeze from the
sea.

MUSICIAN

Pigeon's blood in the gray sky.

(ANTINOUS, EURYMACHUS, *and several other
suitors appear like a hunting pack. They listen a
moment at the closed door then move off together in silence.*)

MUSICIAN

(*To* PROPS.) Bring up the light. (*To audience.*) The
night is gone, and smoothly now, without a pause,
the day light opens up the sky.

(PROPS *goes off: the light comes up slightly;
he returns.*)

PROPS

The drum.

(MUSICIAN *beats an exciting throb, which suddenly ceases.*)

MUSICIAN

(*To* PROPS.) The light. (*To audience.*) The light.
The Crucial Day.

(PROPS *goes off again. Light grows for a moment or two in silence.* PROPS *returns.* TELEMACHUS *slips out of the big doors into the bright light; closes them behind him. He is carefully dressed for the first time. He takes in the bright morning for a moment, then goes off in the direction taken by the suitors. Pause. Brief drum-roll. Enter* AMPHINOMUS *and two other suitors.*)

FIRST SUITOR

The sun is up.

SECOND SUITOR

It'll be a clear day.

FIRST SUITOR

Clear but cool.

(*Pause.*)

AMPHINOMOUS

Antinous and Eurymachus not back yet.

FIRST SUITOR

No.

(*Pause.*)

AMPHINOMUS

If only last night . . . Or there at Zacynthus . . .

FIRST SUITOR

He looks sick.

SECOND SUITOR

What is there to be scared of?

93

AMPHINOMUS

Nothing . . . but look.

(*Enter* EURYMACHUS *and two other suitors.*)

EURYMACHUS

Antinous not back yet?

FIRST SUITOR

No.

AMPHINOMUS

Again!

(*Pause.*)

EURYMACHUS

He wasn't on the beach. Now Antinous is hunting along the cliff path.

AMPHINOMUS

You missed again.

EURYMACHUS

Where would *you* have looked?

(*Enter* ANTINOUS *and the rest.*)

Your fingers are all thumbs.

ANTINOUS

And yours?

(*Pause.*)

EURYMACHUS

Now we'll have to get these out of sight till the moment comes.

(*They hide the weapons in the wings.*)

AMPHINOMUS

This is a bad dream.

(*The men eye him coldly.*)

EURYMACHUS

His guts have turned to whey.

ANTINOUS

Are you with us in this?

AMPHINOMUS

. . . Yes.

(*Short pause. They all focus on a point in the wings.*)

EURYMACHUS

Here he is. Eumaeus with him.

ANTINOUS

Scared.

(*Enter* TELEMACHUS *and* EUMAEUS.)

TELEMACHUS

You go in, Eumaeus. See that everything is ready.

EUMAEUS

I will. (*Looks men over.*) But—

TELEMACHUS

Don't be afraid.

(EUMAEUS *goes in, closing doors behind him.*)

ANTINOUS

I see you've brushed your hair today! Is that why you're so white?

TELEMACHUS

Perhaps.

ANTINOUS

Are you giving a party?

TELEMACHUS

Yes. The last party for my guests. At Penelope's request.

EURYMACHUS

Penelope?

TELEMACHUS

She is yielding today. It only remains to decide to whom. That she leaves to men.

ANTINOUS

Ah . . .

TELEMACHUS

She will surrender Odysseus' great bow to us. Eumaeus is setting up twelve battle-axes in the hall. When my father was here he could shoot an arrow through all twelve eyeholes when the axes were placed in a row. Whoever can do that, she says, shall dispose of her. . . . Don't go. I will bring her now to answer your impatience herself.

(*He goes. Brief pause.*)

AMPHINOMUS

He has some wild hope in this.

EURYMACHUS

She has devised another shroud to entangle us.

ANTINOUS

Or craves to yield at last.

AMPHINOMUS

She may be trying to save Telemachus.

ANTINOUS

Mmm . . . Or else—

EURYMACHUS

What?

ANTINOUS

To leave him to us.

> (*Brief pause. Drum-roll. The men close in to watch where she comes.*)

EURYMACHUS

(*Softly.*) She's bringing it.

AMPHINOMUS

The great bow she kept so long.

ANTINOUS

Shhh . . .

> (*Enter* PENELOPE, TELEMACHUS *and the two women.*)

PENELOPE

Wooers, pretenders: you who have surrounded me, like a helpless captive, with your demands— your time has come at last. Now, as Telemachus has explained, I bring you what you asked for: now you have your way. I tried to avoid this moment. I told you I was waiting for Odysseus, but you wouldn't believe me. The hour has come to bring this weapon forth. For I feel again the terrible spirit of love—which possessed me on my marriage day, which gave me to my husband and my son. You had no right to invoke that spirit. But now I feel it moving again within me, putting my whole life at stake. . . . Where will it carry me? I do not know, but I obey. My things are packed, and I have said good-by to this house, though I'll remember it, I think, to my dying day.

(*She hands the bow to* TELEMACHUS. EURYCLEIA *sobs softly.*)

ANTINOUS

This is a deadly weapon, Penelope.

PENELOPE

Yes.

ANTINOUS

The iron itself, they say, draws a man to it.

PENELOPE

. . . Yes.

(*Pause. The men draw together slightly.*)

ANTINOUS

(*To men.*) Come.

EURYMACHUS

You will take it?

TELEMACHUS

(*Offering bow.*) Take it! Take it!

98

ANTINOUS

(*Disregarding* TELEMACHUS, *to* EURYMACHUS.)
Yes.

EURYMACHUS

We'd fail.

AMPHINOMUS

The bow is useless – a dry branch!

ANTINOUS

(*Very quietly.*) Fools! There are weapons enough
in the house.

TELEMACHUS

(*Who has been trying to hear.*) Useless? (*Laughs
loudly. They stare at him as though he were mad.*)
Why do I laugh – on the day of my mother's grief
and mourning?

AMPHINOMUS

Why, Telemachus?

TELEMACHUS

Because I can succeed or fail – prove myself at last!

(*He tries desperately to string the bow; drum-
roll; enter* ODYSSEUS *and* EUMAEUS. TELEMA-
CHUS *desists.*)

ODYSSEUS

Give me the bow.

ANTINOUS

What do you want?

99

ODYSSEUS

To see whether *I* have the strength of the dead.

AMPHINOMUS

Bitter Penelope! Did you want this? To mock yourself and us with such a wooer among us?

PENELOPE

Yes.

TELEMACHUS

The bow is for me to give!

(*Hands bow to* ODYSSEUS, *who strings it, fits in an arrow, and shoots it over their heads into the wings with an evil whistle.*)

ODYSSEUS

The contest is ready.

ANTINOUS

Let it come.

MEN

(*All together.*) Let it come.

TELEMACHUS

(*To* PENELOPE.) You had better go in.

PENELOPE

Yes.

TELEMACHUS

The rest you are not to see.

PENELOPE

Not to see, but to suffer. (*To* EURYCLEIA.) Come.

(*Drum-roll.* PENELOPE *and* EURYCLEIA *withdraw.*)

TELEMACHUS

(*To* EUMAEUS.) The doors.

(EUMAEUS *opens the doors slightly, to a soft quick drumbeat.* ODYSSEUS, *suitors and* EUMAEUS *file quickly in. Silence.*)

TELEMACHUS

(*One hand on door.*) Eurycleia!

(*She runs back in a crouch, followed at a distance by* EURYNOME, *sobbing.*)

TELEMACHUS

(*Handing her key.*) Lock the doors.

(*He goes in. She double-locks door, starts away to watch. Silence but for sobbing.* EURYCLEIA *near the door,* EURYNOME *to one side, with* PROPS *and* MUSICIAN *downstage, all watch the closed doors.*)

MUSICIAN

(*Quietly.*) Weep your fill.

PROPS

The livid beast

MUSICIAN

Who shakes us now

Won't be denied,

MUSICIAN

Will have his will.

(*War cry from* ODYSSEUS, *followed by yell of despair from all the men.* EURYCLEIA *flies to apply her eye to keyhole then twists back to scream.*)

EURYCLEIA

He! Odysseus! Back from the sea! (*Into keyhole.*) KILL! kill! kill!

(*Violent drum, tumult, yells, doors shaken, silence.*)

(*Softly.*) They can't get away. They have no arms.

(*Tumult again.*)

Again!

(*Tumult.*)

Again!

(*Tumult.*)

Again! Again!

(*Silence.*)

EURYNOME

(*Sobbing.*) No more.

EURYCLEIA

Five left. But his arrows are gone.

Weaponless?

The axes.

(*Screams. Silence.*)

It is the kill.

(*Presently she unlocks the door and opens it slightly.* ODYSSEUS, TELEMACHUS, *and* EUMAEUS *come out.*)

EURYCLEIA

It's over?

ODYSSEUS

All quiet.

EURYCLEIA

(*Clasping his knees.*) Odysseus! Odysseus!

ODYSSEUS

Hush. The dead.

EURYCLEIA

(*To* EURYNOME.) Run—cry that Penelope is delivered!

ODYSSEUS

Sh. . . . Not yet. Some may be hiding.

(*She rises and peers in.*)

ODYSSEUS

Telemachus, have you any will left?

TELEMACHUS

. . . Yes.

ODYSSEUS

The perjured women must be punished. Buried with their lovers. Can you and Eumaeus do it?

TELEMACHUS

Yes.

ODYSSEUS

The house must be purified and put in order. Eurycleia, you and Eurynome see to that.

(TELEMACHUS *and* EUMAEUS *disappear. Then* EURYCLEIA *and* EURYNOME, *then* ODYSSEUS. PROPS *goes off, and the lights dim.*)

MUSICIAN

We are not to see, in there, the price of their faith.

(PROPS *returns. Distant wailing of women.*)

MUSICIAN

It is the wanton women wailing for their own and their lovers' death.

PROPS

The funeral march.

(MUSICIAN *starts a soft, rather quick beat on the drum. We can just glimpse a procession of women, through the half-open door, carrying the dead.*)

Black their grief

But shallow like their youth.

Into the dark with batlike cries

One by one: creature cries: Light, inhuman: one by one.

Black their grief but shallow like their youth.

Let the hurt be brief and not mean much.

> (*The procession is gone, the wailing dies out quickly in the distance. Enter* ODYSSEUS, *followed by the two women.*)

ODYSSEUS

Is the house swept, and the fire lighted on the hearth?

EURYCLEIA

Yes.

> (*Enter* TELEMACHUS, *followed by* EUMAEUS.)

TELEMACHUS

(*Softly.*) What have we killed, so cruelly?

ODYSSEUS

(*Taking his hand.*) Shhh. . . . Go, Eurycleia. Now you may tell Penelope we need her.

> (*She goes.*)

TELEMACHUS

Very still.

ODYSSEUS

Yes.

(*Enter* PENELOPE, *slowly*, *lost*. EURYCLEIA
follows. PENELOPE *comes all the way in in silence
as though afraid to look at* ODYSSEUS.)

TELEMACHUS

Mother! Mother!

PENELOPE

Shh. . . .

TELEMACHUS

Can you say nothing, mother?

PENELOPE

Surely if it were he, I'd know, Telemachus. By certain signs we'd have, we two.

TELEMACHUS

I'm afraid.

ODYSSEUS

That is the lot of mortals on the dark earth. . . .
You've done enough. Take Eumaeus and Eurycleia
and Eurynome; tell the good news. Start music and
dancing. Let the people, if any are watching across the
fields, see our light and hear our song. Let them tell
each other there must be a wedding tonight at the
farm.

(*They go out.*)

ODYSSEUS

We knew each other long ago, Penelope. Our son
is grown into a man. Soon he will be leaving us. We've

gone through much for each other. But not enough. Cold and young you are, as you were before we knew each other. There is no love in our house. Tonight I'll sleep on the floor.

PENELOPE

What can I do? . . . Have them bring Odysseus' bed, at least, for you to sleep on here.

ODYSSEUS

Back to the bitter sea! Our bed—which I myself built into the beams of our room—which no one could move—which no one but you and me was ever to see— our very bed you have pried up and taken away!

PENELOPE

Ah, Odysseus! (*Embracing him.*) The bed is there, just as it used to be! And I—

ODYSSEUS

Ah!

PENELOPE

Ah!

ODYSSEUS

You waited for me.

PENELOPE

There is nothing else.

ODYSSEUS

Life is returning.

PENELOPE

The years are melting. My knees are weak.

ODYSSEUS

(*Yelling strongly into the dark.*) A-ah! Cry! Cry for joy!

> (*Both listen. In a moment a distant cry from* TELEMACHUS *answers.*)

PENELOPE

It was his answer. Our son is back.

> (*Distant singing starts.*)

ODYSSEUS

. . . Come.

> (*They go into the house and disappear;* TELEMACHUS *comes on slowly with* EUMAEUS.)

TELEMACHUS

You were right, Eumaeus. Nothing is lost. Tonight is opening out, continuous with other nights. Nights still before us—far in the future. Nights of childhood. Nothing is lost.

EUMAEUS

Eh? . . . You are a man now.

TELEMACHUS

(*Turning toward the house.*) A cry of joy in the dark. . . . (*He goes slowly toward the house.*) As I was coming through the small grass behind the house.

> (*He goes in.* EUMAEUS *is left downstage peering up, as he was at the beginning of the play.*)

MUSICIAN

(*Softly to* PROPS.) Come.

*(They fold back the doors, then the flats,
which they lean again at the sides of the stage.
Everything has been removed; the stage is empty
as before, except far up near the back wall,*
ODYSSEUS, TELEMACHUS, *and* PENELOPE *clasping*
each other's hands in a gesture of greeting or
*farewell, like a bas-relief on a Greek grave-
stone.)*

PROPS

Hail and farewell. Odysseus. Telemachus. Penelope.

*(The three turn and walk slowly off. The
lights and the offstage singing fade quickly.)*

Curtain

POEMS, 1945-1960

THE AUTUMN GOD: IN TIME OF WAR

The dead grass is bright against
The cloudy mountain, while
Not here, not now, not (only remembered)
Other mountains in former autumns, nor (only
    imagined)
The ultimate dark fields of war.

Each grass-blade, clean, is delicately shining
In the late sunlight, now, here, while
The weather from the north behind the mountain
    announces
The coming of winter. Mindless
The yielding of the creature, in his fur, to slumber;
Belated the gathering, in cold woods, of twigs for
    fuel.
Obedience of other lives to other terror.

Brief and timeless is the sheen
Of the dry grass, seen, unseeing, while
Unseen between the seasons the void
Is void: unreal
Its image of death in the bright spears of grass,
Unreal and trivial (after
The sombre triumphant surrender) as
The detritus of war or pleasure.

AESOP IN HELL: THE FOX AND THE CROW

In the dead-still November woods, a flutter
  in the dry thicket of scrub-oak, betrays
  the crow and his heavy cheese, in harsh struggle,
To reynard-fox's steady, agate gaze.
  The crow's thin claws slip on the branch that
      swings
  and dips, forward and back: how can he raise
The prize, on his weak neck and trembling wings?
  And like unseen, revealing verity,
  the very visage of unwelcome things,
See now the witness of indignity
  glide from behind a bush on noiseless paws,
  with face of ambivalent sympathy.
The crow regains his poise, clenching his claws
  and beak, but his quick breath comes sharp and
      dry
  as the fox holds a tense and lengthy pause.
Then: "I think I could help, if I might try,"
  fox offers in a friendly way, intent
  for signs of weakness in crow's button eye.
"How still and wide now is the whole extent
  of woods and sky! Why, in this tiny copse,
  must our wills lock in grinding punishment?"
Thinks crow, beak locked on cheese; speechlessly
      mopes.
  But to relentless fox his thoughts are clear,
  inspiring more imaginative hopes
Of victory more bitter and more drear
  than scrawny body clamped in his strong teeth:
  the crow's fond spirit downed and clamped in
      fear.
"How beautiful is flight above the heath
  where I must creep, admiring from afar

your gleaming wings," says fox. His face, beneath
Crow's teetering perch, reveals no slightest bar
    to candor or to perfect understanding;
    and now a tell-tale moisture starts to mar
Black crow's bright eye. It is his soul demanding
    the sweets of song, or philosophic solace;
    he is a bird who dreams of human standing.
"How must it feel to leave behind the onus
    of earth-bound creatures, high in air, alone
    with the Alone, in all wide heaven solus?
"I long," fox presses on, "in your own tone
    to hear truth's music—pardon my insistence—
    give me truth's very tune!" That snaps the bone
Of the sad crow's last, desperate resistance,
    unclenches claws and beak, melts him with pity
    for mortal fate, especially in this instance.
Let us not dwell on this absurdity.
    I do not want to hear crow's raucous bawling
    in agony of twisted vanity,
Which, in his disarray, is more appalling
    than living gone. The copse returns to peace,
    in the hushed air one ragged feather falling,
    as though to say that there that scene might cease.

A SUITE FOR WINTER

I

The nights grow cold, and Christmas already here
in the swarming city, city filled with dreams,
lights up streets, bars, shop windows, and my
    fear.
It is the memory of three friends which seems
    (returning at this season every year)
    to chill the city as it roars and gleams.
They come with funeral music, and I hear
    inhuman voices quiring joy unceasing,
    the organ musing on the deathless sphere
Of *Jesu, Joy of Man's Desiring*, freezing
    Kenneth's far gaze and Rachel's inward gaze
    in black and public pageantry, unseeing.
Their son's young face relaxed in death betrays
    their goal: flesh of their flesh, bone of their bone.
    I never see them reach it where it stays
    to claim it for their own and take it home.

II

Behind the traffic the winter stillness
    restores the stillness of that afternoon
    when Rachel, intimate as a long illness,
Draws me into her subtle living-room,
    a harmony composed with her deep guile
    to be her spirit's beautiful cocoon.
"How young we were, too young, when we first
        made trial

116

of marriage, made trial of the great cold town—"
her dark eyes try me, and her knowing smile—
"Yet true, each thought, to what we knew deep
        down."
    Her eyes shine dark in the portrait Sargent made:
    eighteen: hair-ribbons white and white her gown:
Shine still in middle age. "The price we paid
    for things of beauty, 'Rachel's crazy scheme':
    our money spent, our friendships sadly frayed,
I count as nought, however it may seem
    to Kenneth. I have no words: in what I bought
    I put my meaning. But Percy caught that dream
Too soon it seems; too young. Who would have
        thought
    he would have dared the night without a word
    to me? But I keep faith with what he sought
Although the timid church would have preferred
    to call it suicide, bid us despair
    of his short life, leave its real meaning blurred."
Then down the long aisle I see her face go bare,
    her veil thrown back like a black flag flying,
    past the friends' faces she invited there:
Night-creature caught in daylight, bravely trying
    to see past Kenneth moving at her side,
    past his unspoken thought that chokes her crying,
    whereby that pageantry is all belied.

III

Light glows in their house like love, yet it will
        change
    when in the faithless eye of memory
    I see what Percy sees: that love grown strange.
Home for Christmas, stopped in the door, what
        mystery

117

he suddenly confirms he leaves unspoken,
    what tidings of unbearable misery
In the familiar scene; what mocking token:
    his presents piled on the floor, his childhood
        shines
    in timeless light the instant light is broken.
When no open vision exists, the decent signs
    of love: galoshes for snow, white bed for sleep,
    the shining room his mother's dream contrives,
Mean the pale monster gliding in the deep
    of the heart, of the city's unsounded ocean:
    white rendezvous love must and cannot keep.
Faces too firm and fine to show emotion,
    grandfathers' bearded faces, unconfused
    by the sea they defy and its cold commotion;
Young face in which I see his forebears' fused,
    would plumb the times' dark tide with the mortal
        will
    as though, by love's ambiguous light bemused,
    the harpoon's plunge could hold that strange light
        still.

IV

As the time draws near when a man must go
    against his heart, he would, if he could, keep
    his mind subdued to what blank signals show:
The traffic light in motor-throbbing street:
    the needle trembling on the dial: not know
    his goal. So Kenneth would, if he could, meet
The time in the vestry. "Rachel willed it so.
    The church obeyed through cowardice alone.
    My partners come knowing I know they know."
Years fixed on what the evidence has shown:
    years at the law: have weathered Kenneth's face

like Justice' even mask, to a fine stone,
Facing the facts. But when beyond time and space
   the organ music gives the signal, dread
   opens the long course of his losing race.
"All that my partners think and leave unsaid
   is true: Rachel and I must be to blame,
   and the unconventional life we've led.
It's taken me the years since I first came
   to the firm, with Woodrow Wilson's stiff ideal
   of equity, to learn their treacherous game.
Rachel, who never understood, can feel
   alive with painting only, that she craves;
   through it she feels her way to what seems real.
They know we've failed him in their world of
       knaves,
   but the terrible engagement we took on,
   unknown, they cannot know. Each of us saves
An emblem of the love we bore our son,
   Rachel her dream, and I his gun. The price
   is paid, and the blind game is lost, not won."
Then his face moves by Rachel's, held in one vise
   when the confusion of their voices ceases,
   moving in music as in limpid ice
   toward the ferocious goal it never reaches.

V

When the year moves toward cold and dark, the
       city
   denies with its myriad glitter of light
   the primitive chill of terror and pity
Which is the signal of the coming night
   of winter. Curled within its cozy fringe
   of fur, the mindless creature can sleep tight;
But the waking spirit feels the cold impinge

upon the hidden quick of its desire,
night edge its little vision with the tinge
Of boundless dark. What then would it require
to make those gentle faces disappear,
sparks in the black abyss like this brief fire,
Christmas lights that come with the cold of the
    year?

THE WEDDING DAY

Dost thou hear?
Your tale, Sir, would cure deafness.
—*The Tempest*

I

The echoes of your Wedding Day
Whether long past or coming on
Throb deepest when dream feels nearly true
To what we nearly know, near dawn:

Musical, though the tune be gone,
Images beckoning—whence? or where?—
They come from some cord struck in pain
Yet soothe, in sleep, malingering care.

For far below the day's nightmare:
Fond young upon their baffled round,
The aging on those wheels on which
The dry, lost days are shrewdly ground:

To living darkness opened down,
Helpless in sleep's perilous spell,
I hear in the wrinkled human night
Innocent sweetness, chuckling hell,
    That no tongue, fumbling, can retell.

Yet as the great Day gently dawns
—In waking light? In memory?—
The source of dream is actual:
The last dawn on our hustled journey

Together as a family,
Where the too-slowly waking heart

121

Hears the music of your trust
Nearer home, here where we part:

Sounds that mean an early start,
Steps where you softly come and go
As woman lingering, and child,
Obeying music that you know
  Deeper than our lost time, more slow.

II

Come, it is late, the swift approach
Of noontime on your Wedding Day
Has hushed the strange, familiar house,
Taken our musing tune away.

Time now in silence to obey
Only the moment, quickly gone,
Lest we disturb what lived before
Or what's to come; and each alone

Must play a part strange and unknown.
You as the Bride must disappear
With Mother and one trembling Friend,
For He, whom you must not see, is here.

Close in your room what is most dear;
Prepare; but do not seek behind
The small rapt image in the glass
Of child now lost, or woman blind,
  What your love, lost now, comes to find.

But come soon: while we wait downstairs
As nameless Father, Brother, Groom,
We've only our dark suits, routine jokes,
To hide the mystery in your room

Which is our male and jealous doom.
This is no time for our well-dressed dust
To hear its joy cry, or remorse,
And smiling till you come we must

Hold easy fellowship, all our trust
Reflected in that glass: come soon,
For we would hear a woman's voice
Call softly in the light of noon
    That now the time is come: come soon!

III

My eyes fail, though the light of noon
Make every detail clear, and still
As Sunday seemed when I was young,
Or breathless height of a high hill.

Their cars are gone; beyond my will
Your hand's light touch must guide your guide.
Be careful not to muss your dress
In our old car, for our short ride.

With printless step time's high divide
(The village church, the windless dust)
Now cross unseen, unheard, and live
In time to come, as mortals must.

The last steep steps (like death) of trust,
Our ghostly entrance arm-in-arm,
The word, "Who gives?" what none can give.
The word, "Till death" can do no harm

Where nothing lives, while salt and warm,
In spring light welling, in the slow

123

Light of two smiles that lift, that meet,
And sealed as one, now turn, now go,

The mortal sources overflow
In streams that—toward what valley floor?
—Roar blindly downward, gladly lost;
Waters that to spent eyes restore
    The world, more living than before.

IV

To our fond eyes your Wedding Day,
Lingering out its afternoon,
Opens beyond this lawn the world
All echoing your unheard tune:

Mysterious and gentle boon
Of our friends who heard too, confirmed
In the feast they spread beneath high trees,
The sky by moving clouds unfurled,
    That music in the real old world.

In harmony our human world,
Assembling marveling on the lawn:
The young, the old, the crawling child:
Peers wistfully, all-humbly drawn

To offer its welcome and move on;
And as in creature-peace we pass
The riddle of the singing bitch,
The human shadow on the grass,
    Spells out our love in its slow dance.

When the longed-for signal dwarfs our dance
The wider shadow opens far

Beyond what we can see or hear
Night, to our eyes more vast than war,

And your plane, throbbing, spreads before
Remembered faces, side by side,
Lips parted softly, eyes alight,
Love's night, at last. Safe may you ride.

Sounds and scenes of the Day subside
In the frightened silence of the lawn.
In the greedy silence of the heart
Sweet echoes softly go and come:
   The human night is ancient, one.

THE BIG BRANCH: A MEMORANDUM

(For Paul Feeley)

The forgotten country of the Big Branch,
High, to the east of the road up the valley,
Makes no sign on the clear horizon,
Still with the stillness of mountain country.

Fresh as a dream when we first explored it,
Boulder to boulder upstream
In the perilous rush of the cold torrent,
Greedy for trout—the tug, the gleam—

Greedy to see what was above us—
In early sunlight, riffles at play;
In buggy woods, the slow, deep eddies—
Lost, out of time, we climbed all day.

Far up the canyon, dark overtook us.
Our creels were heavy, our feet sore;
In the sudden blackness of the wilderness
The loud gorge deeper than before.

That country, now, looks old, familiar,
And easier. For years we've known,
Through still woods, the trace of a road
Long since washed out and overgrown.

We know that others know the canyon:
By the bridge at its mouth is their picnic-ground:
Wooden tables, beer-cans, turds.
Descending at dusk, sometimes, we've found

That lonesome yokels will gather there,
Sit solemn as rabbits, bolt upright

To down their beer while the blood warms,
Then horse around in the fire-light;

But climb no farther. Between man and gorge
No love is lost: when the rains come
The stream rises with the far-off rumble
Of boulder on boulder, foam and scum

Shoot past on top of a twenty-foot torrent:
A country violated, old,
But savage still. And in fine weather,
Climbing upstream again in the cold

Clear water, the delicate fly
On the swirling pool will still bring answer
From the wild and living spirit of the stream:
Trout, a flicker of salmon and silver.

After a breathless plunge at noon,
On a sunny ledge, spread out to dry,
We can loaf in prehuman emptiness,
Lost, out of time, though time goes by.

THE BOOKSTORE, EVENING

(*After Baudelaire*)

Une atmosphère obscure enveloppe la ville,
Aux uns portant la paix, aux autres le souci.

At dusk the pervasive hum of the city
Changes in timbre, as motors of trucks and buses,
Speeding past crossings, sound the night motive.
Crowds are released, and with closed faces go—
Waiting, then dodging—the weaving ways of
     evening's
Logic and necessity. Far up the long
And dimming traffic-canyon you can see
Lights coming out, love's countless foci.

Much is known of what moves in the city
From year to year, from hour to hour. Clues
On the analogy of late Roman times,
Equations based on discount rates or ohms,
Blueprints of reflex acts or restless dreams,
Can quiet the mind, withdrawn at dusk, that knows
What scheme will reassure it.

                Turn away,
Follow the next dark side-street. There,
Past "Diamonds" past "Vienna Bakery"
Past closed "Men's Furnishings" the aqueous light
Of the bookstore's silent-shining windows draws
Shadowy passersby to pause and gaze:
Symbolic Logic—Streetcar Named Desire—
Iconography—The Reign of Nero—
Superheterodyne Converters—Zen—

Diseases of Malnutrition—Probability—
Erotica—The World
As Will and Idea—
Will seem to flicker briefly as they meet
The eye, then die as the contact breaks, and lie
Cold under glass. Unseen, unheard
As live things in the night below the ocean,
The bodiless swarming of the city's minds,
Each on its filament of meaning, choosing
The form of pleasure or power which will live
Tonight in its brief devotion. Who can say,
"Nothing human is strange to me"?

                Who imagine
The mathematical fraternities
On long, centrifugal tips of thinking, wooing
Their incommensurate geometries?
Marvels of ingenuity must be looming
On grids too thin for minds that chill and tire:
This very night, outside night's audible doings,
A mind immune, tuned on intricate wire,
May know miraculously close and seal
Its "circuit and subterfuge of thought and desire":
Its calculus confirm—undreamed-of, cosmic, real—
What nothing human can conceive or feel.

"Sois sage, ô ma Douleur, et tiens-toi plus
    tranquille."
Why should you fret or shudder? for you know
That in this window wait alluringly
Day-dreams devised with foresight to bemuse
In circuits short, imaginable, easy,
Every nocturnal need. See, you may choose
That cosy British murder-mystery,

And in its comfortable prose enclosed,
With its well-spoken, harmless elderly,
Sink safely toward the one sure goal
That's figured sleepily in night's deep hole.
Not "ohm" but "home" shall hum the night of the
    city.